WELCOME TO THE U.S.A.
CONNECTICUT

Written by Ann Heinrichs   Illustrated by Matt Kania
Content Adviser: Jon Emmett Purmont, EdD, Professor of History,
Southern Connecticut State University, New Haven, Connecticut

The Child's World

Published in the United States of America by The Child's World®
PO Box 326 • Chanhassen, MN 55317-0326
800-599-READ • www.childsworld.com

Photo Credits
Cover: Getty Images/The Image Bank/Michael Melford; frontispiece: Getty Images/Taxi/Gary Buss.

Interior: American Clock & Watch Museum: 18; Coastal Fairfield County Convention & Visitors Bureau: 38; Corbis: 12 (Lee Snider/Photo Images), 26 (Dale C. Spartas), 29 (Yogi, Inc.), 30 (Phil Schermeister), 34 (Louie Psihoyos); Essex Steam Train & Riverboat: 6; Getty Images/Hulton|Archive/MPI: 13; Robert Hakalski/Mashantucket Pequot Museum: 10; Library of Congress: 15, 32; Peg Limbacher/St. Andrew's Society of Connecticut: 17; Mark Twain House & Museum: 33; James Marshall/Corbis: 9, 14, 25.

Acknowledgments
The Child's World®: Mary Berendes, Publishing Director

Editorial Directions, Inc.: E. Russell Primm, Editorial Director; Katie Marsico, Associate Editor; Judith Shiffer, Assistant Editor; Matt Messbarger, Editorial Assistant; Susan Hindman, Copy Editor; Melissa McDaniel, Proofreader; Kevin Cunningham, Peter Garnham, Matt Messbarger, Olivia Nellums, Chris Simms, Molly Symmonds, Katherine Trickle, Carl Stephen Wender, Fact Checkers; Tim Griffin/IndexServ, Indexer; Cian Loughlin O'Day, Photo Researcher and Editor

The Design Lab: Kathleen Petelinsek, Design and art production

Library of Congress Cataloging-in-Publication Data
Heinrichs, Ann.
    Connecticut / by Ann Heinrichs.
      p. cm. — (Welcome to the U.S.A.)
    Includes index.
    ISBN 1-59296-442-7 (library bound : alk. paper) 1. Connecticut—Juvenile literature.
I. Title.
    F94.3.H453 2006
    974.6—dc22   2005000518

Ann Heinrichs is the author of more than 100 books for children and young adults. She has also enjoyed successful careers as a children's book editor and an advertising copywriter. Ann grew up in Fort Smith, Arkansas, and lives in Chicago, Illinois.

About the Author
Ann Heinrichs

Matt Kania loves maps and, as a kid, dreamed of making them. In school he studied geography and cartography, and today he makes maps for a living. Matt's favorite thing about drawing maps is learning about the places they represent. Many of the maps he has created can be found in books, magazines, videos, Web sites, and public places.

About the Map Illustrator
Matt Kania

On the cover: Ride the ferris wheel at the fair in Hartford.
On page one: Connecticut's forests display beautiful colors every fall.

OUR CONNECTICUT TRIP

Connecticut's Nicknames: The Constitution State, the Nutmeg State, and the Provision State

What's going on in Connecticut today? Let's take a tour and see! You'll find plenty to explore there. You'll wander through whaling ships and submarines. You'll see dinosaurs, beaver homes, and donkey shows. You'll watch giant balloons floating down the street. And you'll meet Mark Twain and Nathan Hale. Not bad for such a tiny state!

Are you ready to roll? Then buckle up and hang on tight. We're off to see Connecticut!

WELCOME TO CONNECTICUT

As you travel through Connecticut, watch for all the interesting facts along the way.

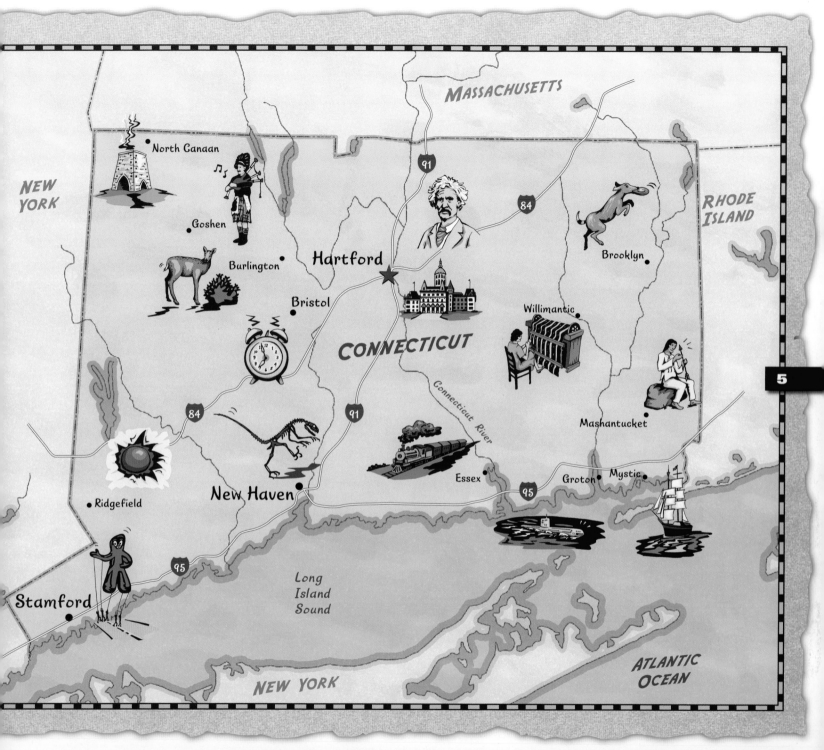

NEW YORK

MASSACHUSETTS

RHODE ISLAND

North Canaan

Goshen

Burlington

Bristol

Hartford

CONNECTICUT

Brooklyn

Willimantic

Mashantucket

84

91

84

91

Connecticut River

New Haven

Essex

Groton

Mystic

95

95

Ridgefield

Stamford

Long Island Sound

NEW YORK

ATLANTIC OCEAN

5

Riding the Essex Steam Train

Next stop—Connecticut River Valley! Explore this region while riding the Essex Steam Train.

HIGHEST AND LOWEST POINTS
Highest: The south slope of Mount Frissell at 2,380 feet (725 m)
Lowest: Sea level along the Long Island Sound

All aboard for the Essex Steam Train! Puffy steam clouds pour from the smokestack. Soon you're chugging through the countryside. What a way to explore the Connecticut River Valley!

The Connecticut River flows through central Connecticut. It empties into Long Island Sound. That's part of the Atlantic Ocean. Connecticut's whole southern border is a seacoast. Fishing and sailing are big parts of Connecticut's history.

Much of Connecticut is hilly. Deep river valleys cut through the hills. The Taconic Mountains reach into northwest Connecticut. This is the state's highest region. The land here is wild and rugged.

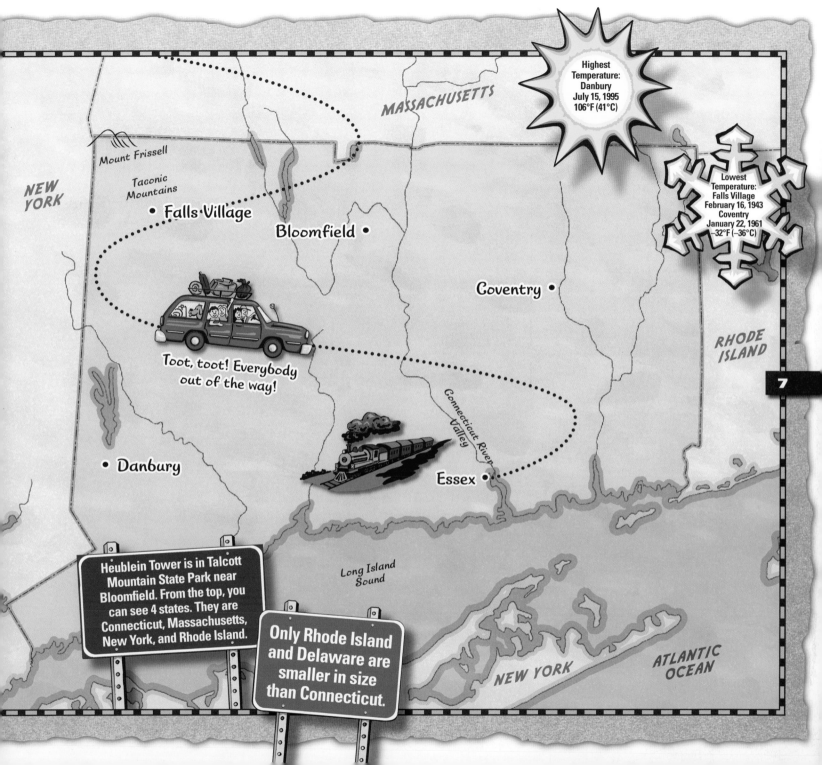

MASSACHUSETTS

NEW YORK

Mount Frissell

Taconic Mountains

• Falls Village

Bloomfield •

Coventry •

RHODE ISLAND

Highest Temperature: Danbury July 15, 1995 106°F (41°C)

Lowest Temperature: Falls Village February 16, 1943 Coventry January 22, 1961 −32°F (−36°C)

Toot, toot! Everybody out of the way!

Connecticut River Valley

• Danbury

Essex •

Long Island Sound

Heublein Tower is in Talcott Mountain State Park near Bloomfield. From the top, you can see 4 states. They are Connecticut, Massachusetts, New York, and Rhode Island.

Only Rhode Island and Delaware are smaller in size than Connecticut.

NEW YORK

ATLANTIC OCEAN

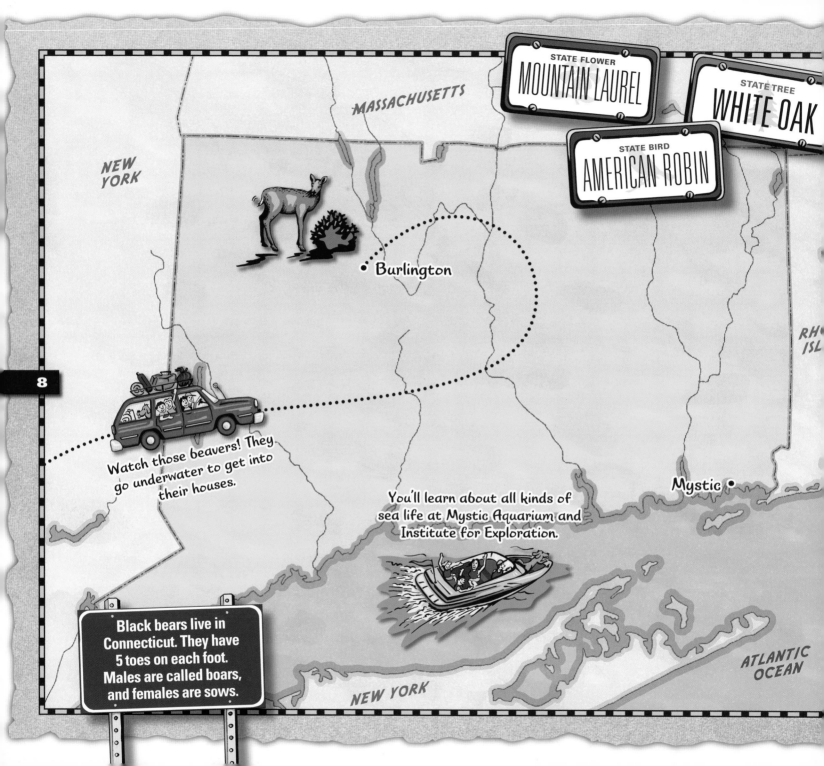

STATE FLOWER
MOUNTAIN LAUREL

STATE TREE
WHITE OAK

STATE BIRD
AMERICAN ROBIN

MASSACHUSETTS

NEW YORK

RHODE ISLAND

Burlington

Watch those beavers! They go underwater to get into their houses.

You'll learn about all kinds of sea life at Mystic Aquarium and Institute for Exploration.

Mystic

Black bears live in Connecticut. They have 5 toes on each foot. Males are called boars, and females are sows.

ATLANTIC OCEAN

NEW YORK

Wildlife at Sessions Woods

Have you ever seen a beaver lodge? Just visit Sessions Woods Wildlife Management Area. It's near Burlington. You'll see these amazing, cone-shaped beaver houses. Beavers build them with sticks, grass, and mud.

Keep wandering through the woods. You'll see chipmunks, turtles, and frogs. You'll meet some white-tailed deer, too.

Many animals make their homes in Connecticut's forests. They include foxes, skunks, rabbits, and raccoons. Sometimes a snowy owl hoots in the trees.

Gulls, sandpipers, and terns live by the shore. Plenty of shellfish live offshore, too. There are clams, oysters, scallops, and lobsters. People love to eat them!

Ribbit! Connecticut is home to several types of frogs and toads.

The National Park Service has 3 sites in Connecticut.

Mashantucket Pequot Museum

Want to know how Native Americans once hunted caribou? Visit Mashantucket Pequot Museum!

Connecticut colonists adopted the Fundamental Orders in 1639. This was a type of constitution, or basic set of laws. That's why Connecticut is called the Constitution State.

Stroll through Mashantucket Pequot Museum. Its life-size scenes teach visitors about the Pequot culture. The Pequot people lived in Connecticut hundreds of years ago. You'll learn how they built homes and canoes. You'll see how they cooked, hunted, and played.

English **colonists** were Connecticut's first white settlers. They founded Windsor in 1633. Windsor and other new towns formed the Connecticut **Colony.** It was one of England's thirteen American colonies.

Early colonists were farmers. Some also hunted and fished for food. Manufacturing began as early as the 1700s. Connecticut factories made clocks, ships, and silver goods.

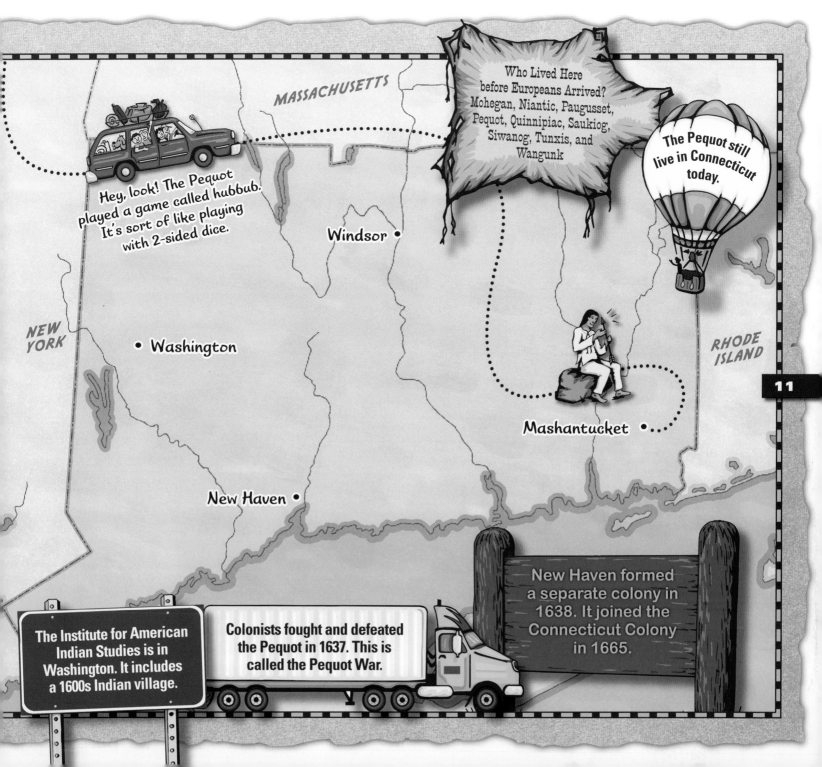

MASSACHUSETTS

Hey, look! The Pequot played a game called hubbub. It's sort of like playing with 2-sided dice.

Who Lived Here before Europeans Arrived? Mohegan, Niantic, Paugusset, Pequot, Quinnipiac, Saukiog, Siwanog, Tunxis, and Wangunk

The Pequot still live in Connecticut today.

Windsor •

NEW YORK

• Washington

RHODE ISLAND

Mashantucket •

New Haven •

The Institute for American Indian Studies is in Washington. It includes a 1600s Indian village.

Colonists fought and defeated the Pequot in 1637. This is called the Pequot War.

New Haven formed a separate colony in 1638. It joined the Connecticut Colony in 1665.

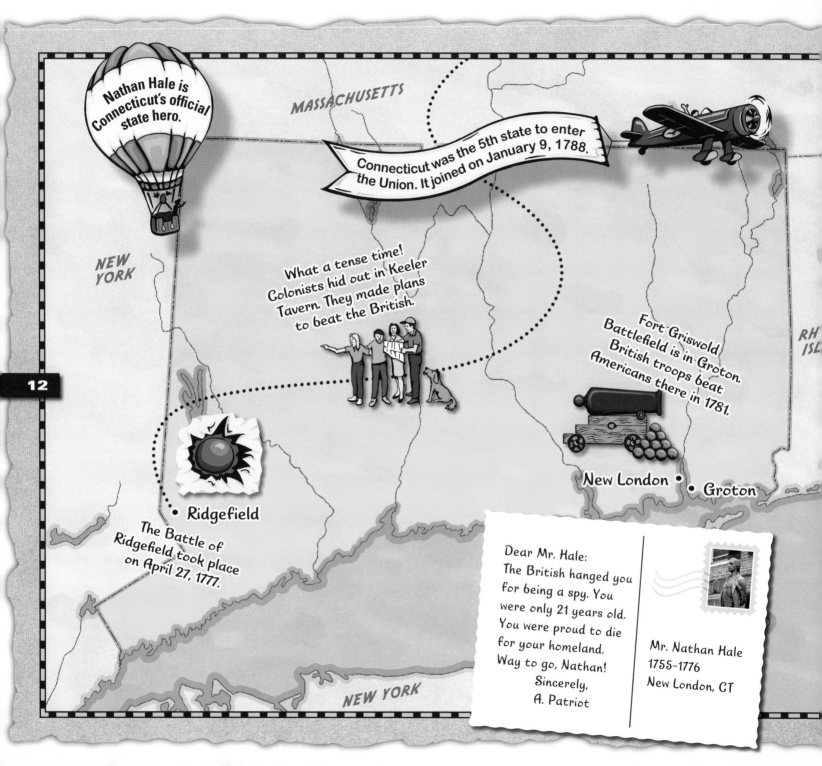

Nathan Hale is Connecticut's official state hero.

MASSACHUSETTS

Connecticut was the 5th state to enter the Union. It joined on January 9, 1788.

NEW YORK

What a tense time! Colonists hid out in Keeler Tavern. They made plans to beat the British.

Fort Griswold Battlefield is in Groton. British troops beat Americans there in 1781.

RH ISL

New London • Groton

• Ridgefield

The Battle of Ridgefield took place on April 27, 1777.

NEW YORK

Dear Mr. Hale:
The British hanged you for being a spy. You were only 21 years old. You were proud to die for your homeland. Way to go, Nathan!
Sincerely,
A. Patriot

Mr. Nathan Hale
1755–1776
New London, CT

Ridgefield's Keeler Tavern and the Revolutionary War

In time, colonists grew sick of British rule. They decided to fight for their freedom. They fought the British in the Revolutionary War (1775–1783). Nathan Hale of Connecticut was a war hero.

One battle took place in Ridgefield. The British shot at Keeler **Tavern.** A British cannonball is still stuck there! Just stop by, and you can see it. That tavern is now a museum. The museum's guides wear colonial clothing.

How did the war turn out? The colonists won! Then the colonies became the first thirteen states.

Hooray for Nathan Hale! This famous patriot was a Connecticut resident.

England is now part of Great Britain. *English* and *British* are often used to mean the same thing.

This old textile mill is located in Wauregan.

14

Mills stood alongside a river. The flowing water turned a mill wheel. That powered the mill's machine parts.

Roam around the Mill Museum. You'll begin to see how mill workers lived. Mills were early factories. People worked there twelve or more hours a day. Even children worked in the mills.

You'll see a mill worker's house. You'll also see the company store. Workers bought their food and clothes there.

Willimantic's mill made cotton thread and cloth. Eli Whitney invented the cotton gin in 1793. It removed seeds from cotton. Then people could make cotton goods faster. Whitney also built a gun factory in Hamden. Connecticut became a leading factory state. Its factories made cloth, rubber, shoes, and much more.

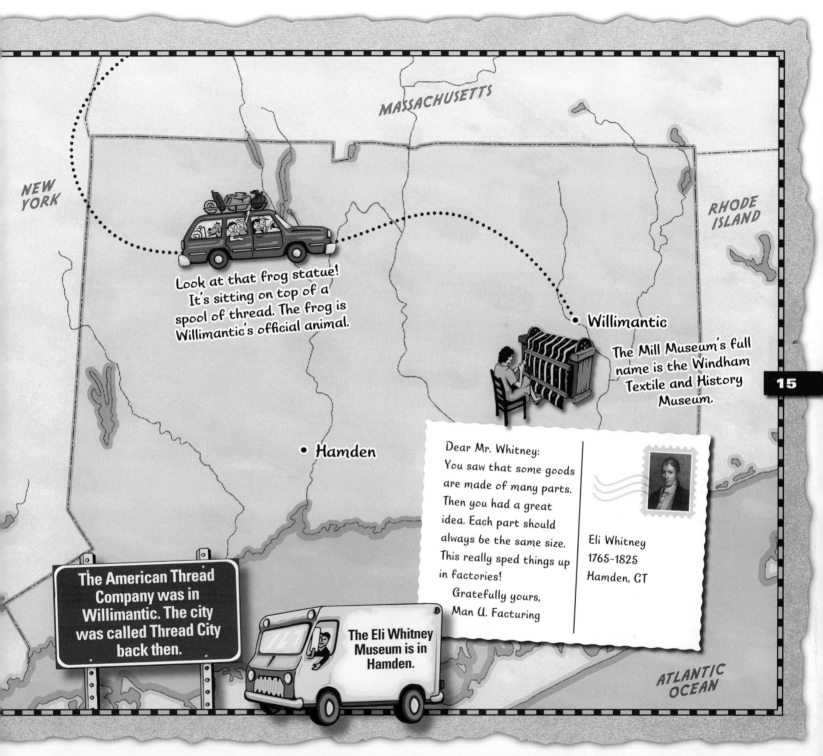

MASSACHUSETTS

NEW YORK

RHODE ISLAND

Look at that frog statue! It's sitting on top of a spool of thread. The frog is Willimantic's official animal.

• Willimantic

The Mill Museum's full name is the Windham Textile and History Museum.

• Hamden

Dear Mr. Whitney:
You saw that some goods are made of many parts. Then you had a great idea. Each part should always be the same size. This really sped things up in factories!
Gratefully yours,
Man U. Facturing

Eli Whitney
1765-1825
Hamden, CT

The American Thread Company was in Willimantic. The city was called Thread City back then.

The Eli Whitney Museum is in Hamden.

ATLANTIC OCEAN

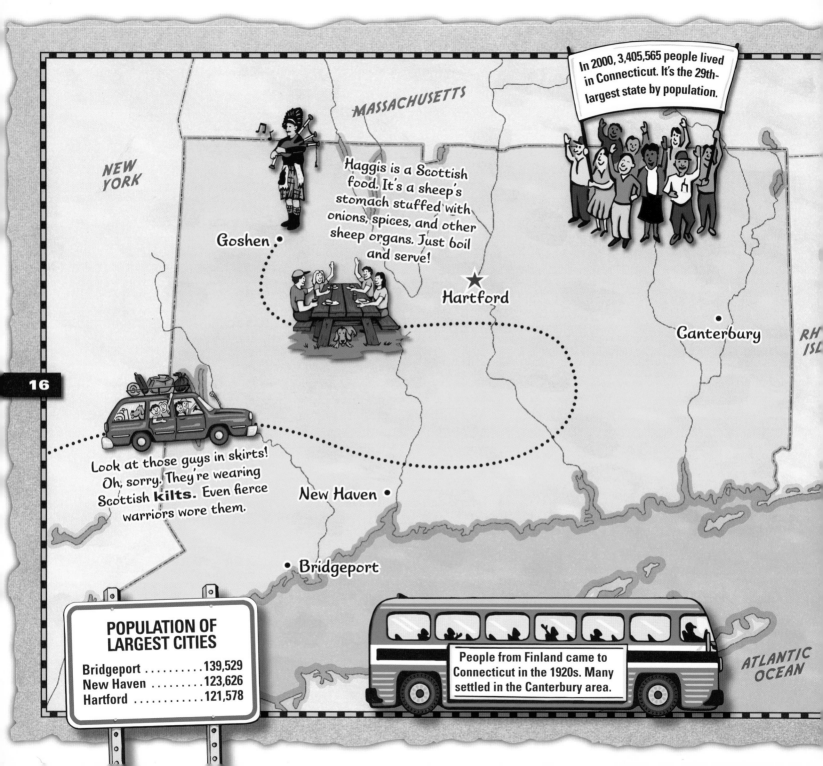

NEW YORK

MASSACHUSETTS

In 2000, 3,405,565 people lived in Connecticut. It's the 29th-largest state by population.

Haggis is a Scottish food. It's a sheep's stomach stuffed with onions, spices, and other sheep organs. Just boil and serve!

Goshen •

★ Hartford

Canterbury •

RH ISL

Look at those guys in skirts! Oh, sorry. They're wearing Scottish **kilts.** Even fierce warriors wore them.

New Haven •

• Bridgeport

POPULATION OF LARGEST CITIES

Bridgeport 139,529
New Haven 123,626
Hartford 121,578

People from Finland came to Connecticut in the 1920s. Many settled in the Canterbury area.

ATLANTIC OCEAN

Join the fun at the Scottish Festival. You can enter different athletic events. All of them are originally from Scotland. There are also piping competitions. Watch as expert bagpipers play their hearts out!

This festival celebrates Scottish culture. Highland dancers perform some of the world's oldest folk dances. Scottish sheepdogs show off their skills. And there's lots of Scottish food.

People from Scotland were early settlers in Connecticut. Other settlers were from England. Many **immigrants** came to work in the mills. Some arrived from Ireland or Canada. Others came from Italy, Poland, Germany, or Russia. They all made new homes in Connecticut.

The Scottish Festival includes contests for kids, too! These children search for coins in a haystack.

17

Tick tock, tick tock. Make time to stop by Bristol's Clock and Watch Museum!

What time is it? Just look around. You'll see what time it is—1,500 times! You're at the American Clock and Watch Museum. This museum has more than 1,500 clocks and watches. You'll see grandfather clocks. You'll see clocks for shelves and walls. Check out the Mickey Mouse watches. There are Porky Pig and Bugs Bunny watches, too!

Some clocks used to be in factories. They punched the workers' "in and out" times. Other clocks came from railroad stations or church towers. Just wait till the big hand reaches twelve on each one. You'll get to hear all the chimes!

Eli Terry (1772–1852) was a great Connecticut clockmaker. He had clock factories in Plymouth and Thomaston.

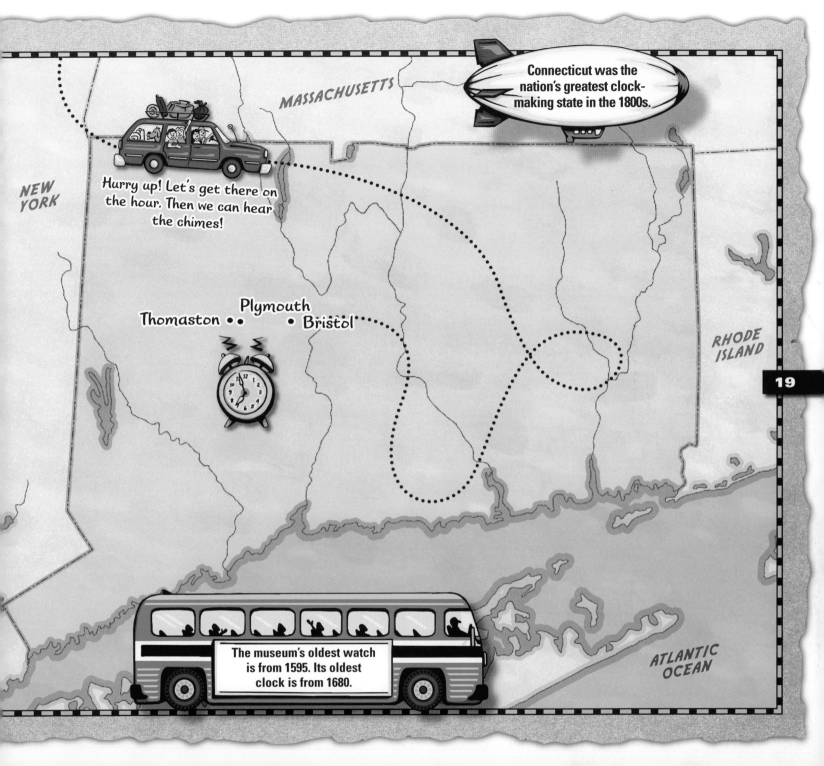

Connecticut was the nation's greatest clock-making state in the 1800s.

Hurry up! Let's get there on the hour. Then we can hear the chimes!

NEW YORK

MASSACHUSETTS

Thomaston • • Plymouth • Bristol

RHODE ISLAND

The museum's oldest watch is from 1595. Its oldest clock is from 1680.

ATLANTIC OCEAN

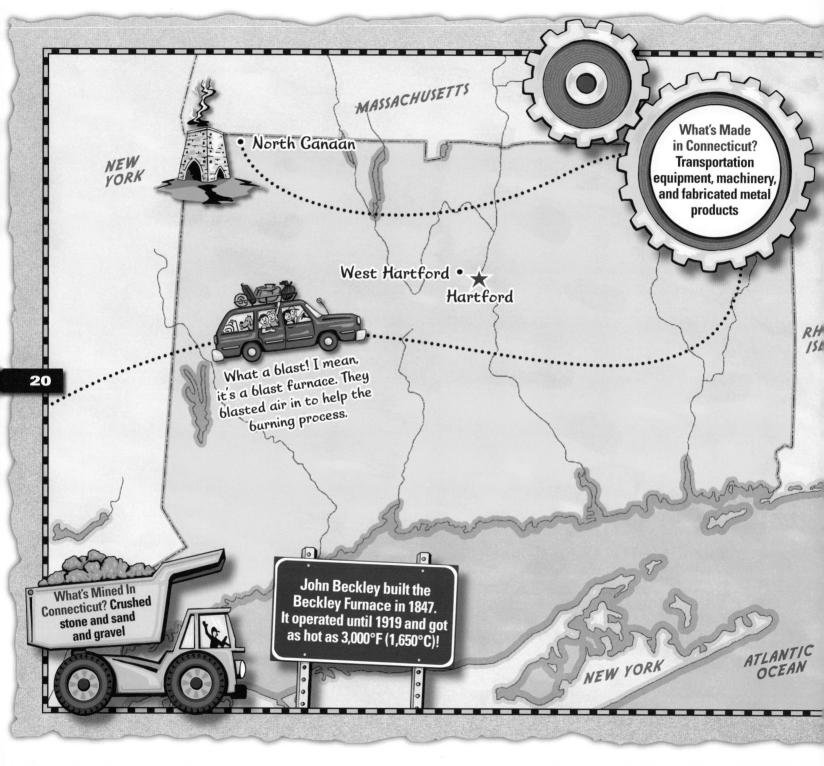

MASSACHUSETTS

NEW YORK

North Canaan

What's Made in Connecticut? Transportation equipment, machinery, and fabricated metal products

West Hartford •

★ Hartford

What a blast! I mean, it's a blast furnace. They blasted air in to help the burning process.

RH ISL

What's Mined In Connecticut? Crushed stone and sand and gravel

John Beckley built the Beckley Furnace in 1847. It operated until 1919 and got as hot as 3,000°F (1,650°C)!

NEW YORK

ATLANTIC OCEAN

Beckley Furnace in North Canaan

You might have a **furnace** where you live. It produces heat to keep you warm. The Beckley Furnace was a different kind of furnace. People used it to melt iron. That iron was made into train car wheels.

You can stand inside the furnace if you like. Don't worry. It's not burning anymore!

Iron was an important factory product in the 1800s. Today, Connecticut factories still make things with metal. They produce knives, tools, and other metal goods.

Many factories make things for the U.S. government. They build submarines, helicopters, and airplane parts. Connecticut makes medicine, soap, and computers, too.

A worker fashions a gun at the Colt Factory in West Hartford.

Ships ahoy! Visitors explore a ship at Mystic Seaport.

Whaling Days at Mystic Seaport

Want to go below deck on a real whaling ship? Then head to Mystic Seaport! It's built just like an old coastal village.

Whaling was a big **industry** in the 1800s. Only Connecticut's cloth and shoe industries employed more people. Mystic was known for both whaling and shipbuilding.

Whalers sailed out to sea in big ships. They often stayed out for weeks. The whales they brought back had many uses. Whale blubber, or fat, was made into oil. People burned the oil in lamps.

You can climb aboard the *Charles W. Morgan* at Mystic. It was the world's last wooden whaling ship.

Whale oil was burned in streetlights, lighthouses, and train headlights!

Ambergris (AM-bur-gris) comes from whale intestines. It was used to make perfume.

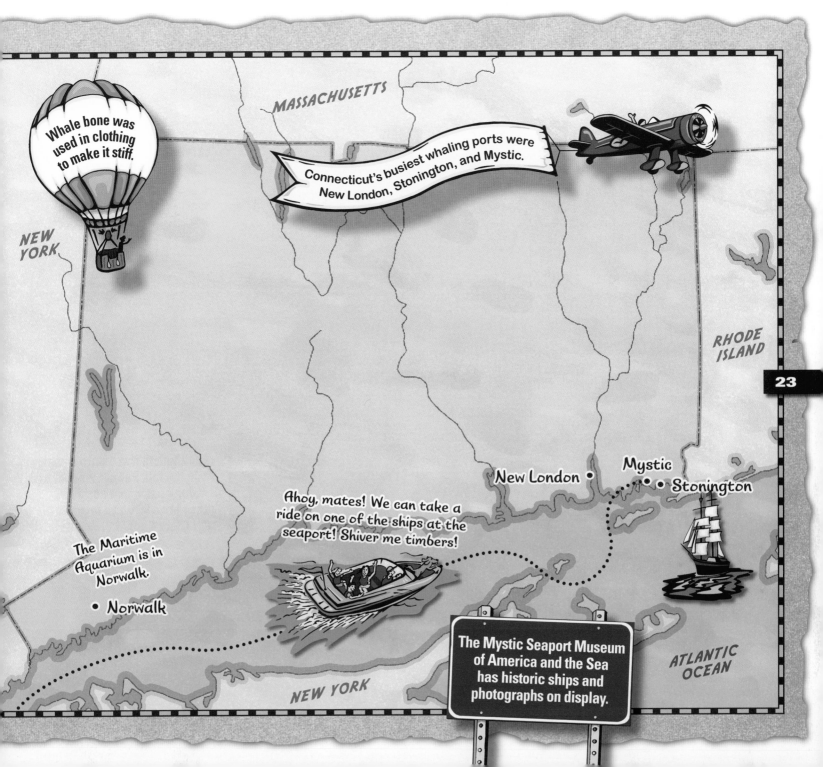

MASSACHUSETTS

Whale bone was used in clothing to make it stiff.

Connecticut's busiest whaling ports were New London, Stonington, and Mystic.

NEW YORK

RHODE ISLAND

New London • Mystic • Stonington

Ahoy, mates! We can take a ride on one of the ships at the seaport! Shiver me timbers!

The Maritime Aquarium is in Norwalk.

• Norwalk

The Mystic Seaport Museum of America and the Sea has historic ships and photographs on display.

NEW YORK

ATLANTIC OCEAN

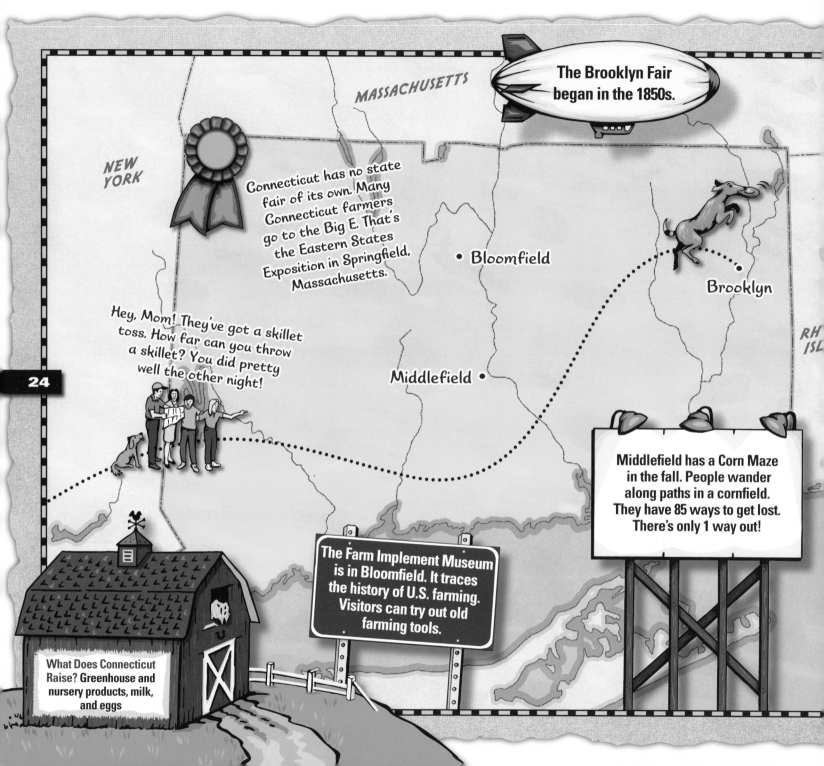

24

The Brooklyn Fair began in the 1850s.

MASSACHUSETTS

NEW YORK

Connecticut has no state fair of its own. Many Connecticut farmers go to the Big E. That's the Eastern States Exposition in Springfield, Massachusetts.

Bloomfield

Brooklyn

RH ISL

Hey, Mom! They've got a skillet toss. How far can you throw a skillet? You did pretty well the other night!

Middlefield

Middlefield has a Corn Maze in the fall. People wander along paths in a cornfield. They have 85 ways to get lost. There's only 1 way out!

The Farm Implement Museum is in Bloomfield. It traces the history of U.S. farming. Visitors can try out old farming tools.

What Does Connecticut Raise? Greenhouse and nursery products, milk, and eggs

Do you like farm fairs? Then try the Brooklyn Fair. You've never seen anything like it! It's got a donkey show. There are dog tricks and lawn mower races. There's a contest for dogs, too. The prettiest, ugliest, and silliest dogs get prizes!

Connecticut doesn't have much farmland. But farmers make the most of it. Some grow shrubs and flowers for people's yards. Some raise dairy cattle for their milk. Others raise chickens that lay eggs. Hay, corn, and tobacco are important crops.

People go fishing for seafood, too. They catch lobsters, oysters, crabs, and clams. Of course, they also catch fish.

How about a glass of milk? Connecticut farmers raise dairy cows.

25

What Are Connecticut's Fishing Products?
Lobsters, oysters, and bluefish

Do you enjoy fishing? Then Connecticut is the state for you!

The Barnum Museum in Bridgeport focuses on the life of circus king P. T. Barnum.

Stamford's Giant Balloon Parade

Here comes Gumby. There goes Miss Piggy. And there's Rocky and Bullwinkle. It's the Giant Balloon Parade!

Stamford holds this parade close to Thanksgiving. The giant balloons are too cool! They're way above everybody's heads.

You can have plenty of fun in Connecticut. There are boat races and craft shows. In the winter, people enjoy skiing and sleigh rides.

The forests are great for hiking and camping. Some people prefer the seashore. They swim, fish, and collect seashells.

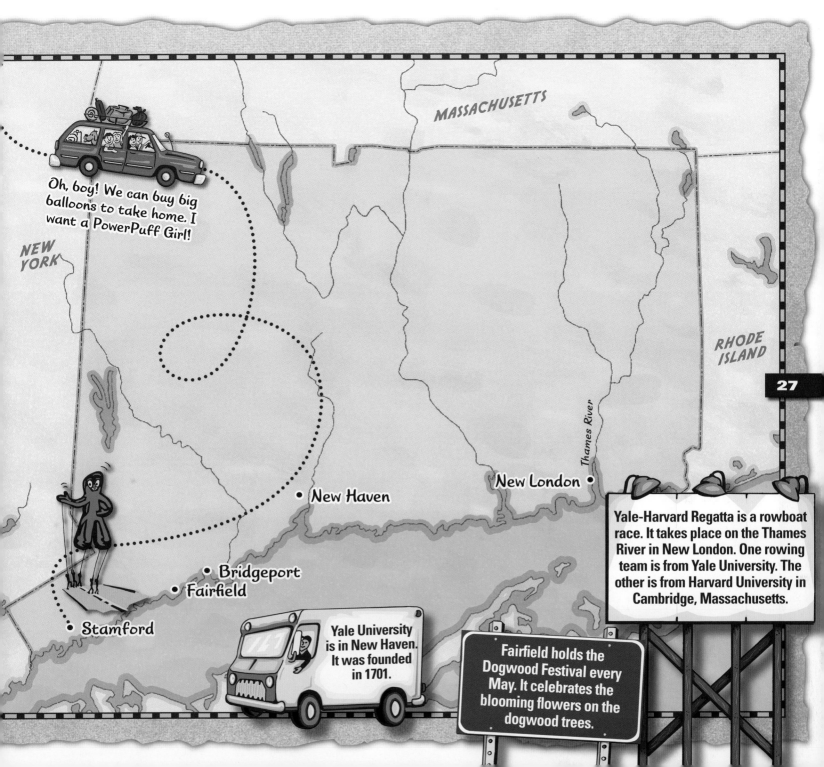

Oh, boy! We can buy big balloons to take home. I want a PowerPuff Girl!

MASSACHUSETTS

NEW YORK

RHODE ISLAND

Thames River

New London •

• New Haven

• Bridgeport

• Fairfield

• Stamford

Yale University is in New Haven. It was founded in 1701.

Fairfield holds the Dogwood Festival every May. It celebrates the blooming flowers on the dogwood trees.

Yale-Harvard Regatta is a rowboat race. It takes place on the Thames River in New London. One rowing team is from Yale University. The other is from Harvard University in Cambridge, Massachusetts.

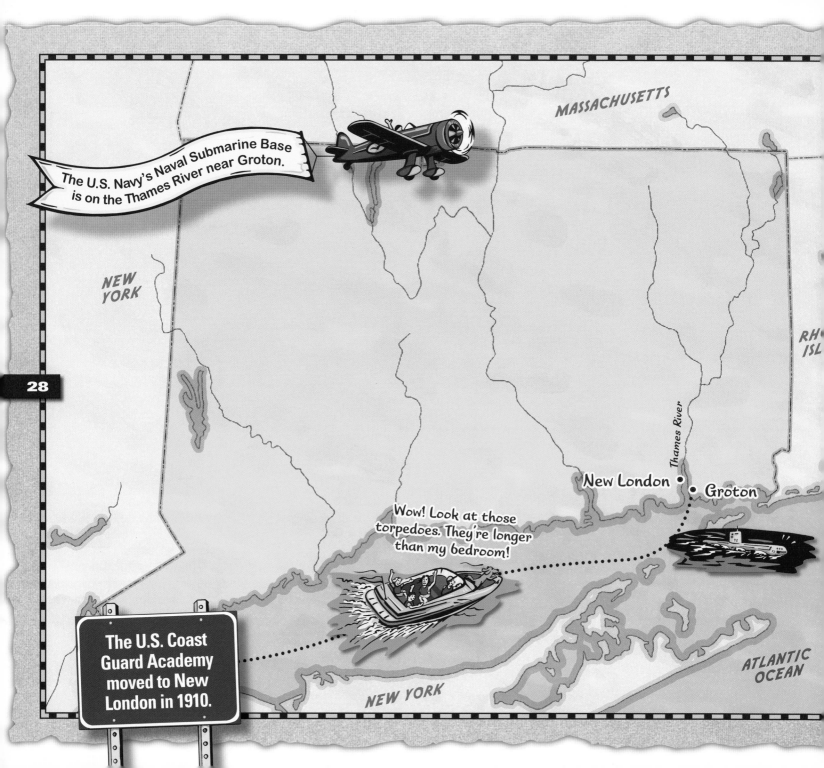

MASSACHUSETTS

The U.S. Navy's Naval Submarine Base is on the Thames River near Groton.

NEW YORK

RH ISL

Thames River

New London • • Groton

Wow! Look at those torpedoes. They're longer than my bedroom!

The U.S. Coast Guard Academy moved to New London in 1910.

ATLANTIC OCEAN

NEW YORK

You'll love touring the submarine USS *Nautilus*. First, you enter the **torpedo** room. Next, you see where the sailors slept. They had bunk beds, showers, and toilets. Finally, you visit the attack center. That's where sailors spotted targets and fired torpedoes.

The *Nautilus* was the first **nuclear**-powered submarine. It's docked at Groton, where it was built.

Connecticut began building submarines in the 1920s. Business sped up during World War II (1939–1945). Connecticut made many kinds of war supplies. These included submarines, airplane parts, and **ammunition.** Everyone was proud of the USS *Nautilus*. It was first launched in 1954.

Would you make a good sailor? Tour the USS *Nautilus* and find out!

Groton's Submarine Force Museum is next to the *Nautilus*. It has the world's finest collection of submarine items.

Wow! That dome is covered with a thin layer of real gold!

The state capitol is very fancy. It almost looks like a castle. Some corners have pointy towers. The tallest tower is in the center. There's a golden dome on top. The dome sparkles in the sunlight!

Many government offices are in the capitol. Connecticut's government has three branches. One branch makes the state's laws. It's called the General Assembly. Another branch carries out those laws. It's headed by the governor. Courts make up the third branch. They decide whether someone has broken the law.

30

Stop by the capitol in Hartford. Connecticut lawmakers work there.

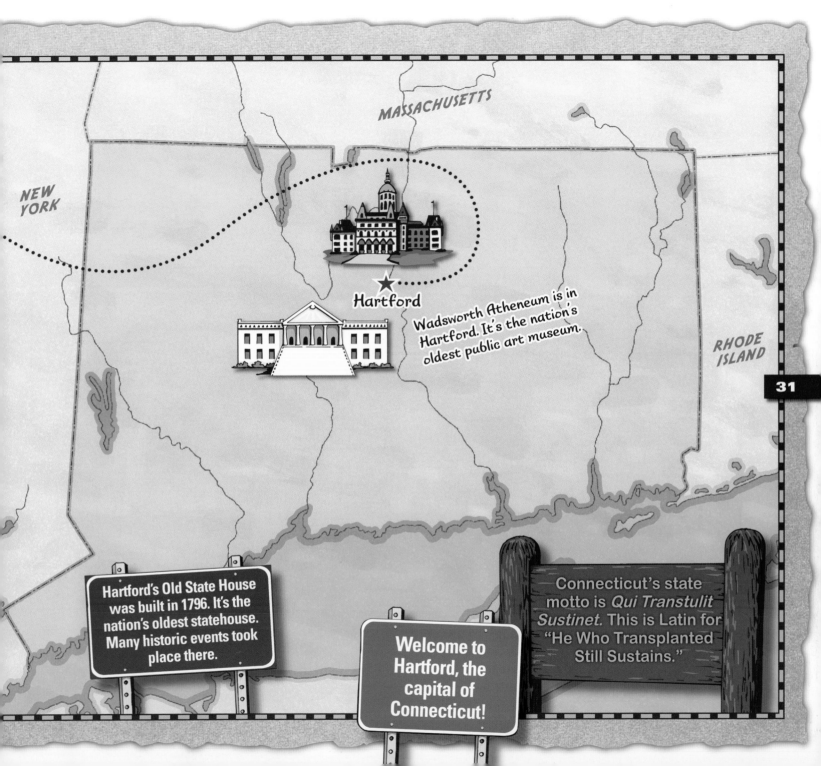

MASSACHUSETTS

NEW YORK

RHODE ISLAND

★
Hartford

Wadsworth Atheneum is in Hartford. It's the nation's oldest public art museum.

Hartford's Old State House was built in 1796. It's the nation's oldest statehouse. Many historic events took place there.

Welcome to Hartford, the capital of Connecticut!

Connecticut's state motto is *Qui Transtulit Sustinet.* This is Latin for "He Who Transplanted Still Sustains."

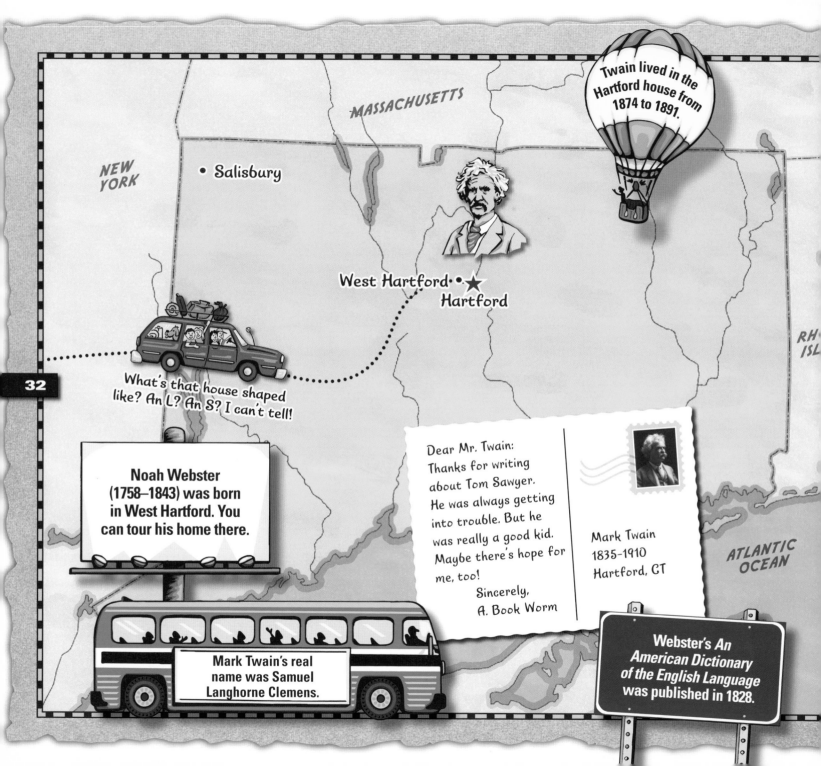

MASSACHUSETTS

NEW YORK

• Salisbury

Twain lived in the Hartford house from 1874 to 1891.

West Hartford • ★ Hartford

RH ISL

What's that house shaped like? An L? An S? I can't tell!

Noah Webster (1758–1843) was born in West Hartford. You can tour his home there.

Dear Mr. Twain:
Thanks for writing about Tom Sawyer. He was always getting into trouble. But he was really a good kid. Maybe there's hope for me, too!
Sincerely,
A. Book Worm

Mark Twain
1835–1910
Hartford, CT

ATLANTIC OCEAN

Mark Twain's real name was Samuel Langhorne Clemens.

Webster's *An American Dictionary of the English Language* was published in 1828.

Mark Twain's House in Hartford

The 1st public library in Connecticut opened in Salisbury in 1810.

Windows and chimneys are sticking out everywhere. But where are the doors? It's hard to know where to go in!

This odd house belonged to author Mark Twain. He wrote many books there. One was *The Adventures of Tom Sawyer*. Another was *The Adventures of Huckleberry Finn*. Kids enjoy these stories. They show how children might have lived long ago.

Noah Webster was another famous person from Connecticut. He put together the first dictionary. It had thousands of words in it!

Have you read any of Mark Twain's stories? Be sure to visit his house in Hartford!

Dinosaurs at the Peabody Museum

How big were dinosaurs? Try walking around in a room full of them. Just visit the Peabody Museum of Natural History. It's at Yale University in New Haven.

The Peabody's Great Hall of Dinosaurs is awesome. Dinosaur skeletons are everywhere. You'll see just how big those monsters were. You'd barely come up to their knees!

You'll also see saber-toothed cats. They had long, pointy teeth. There are skeletons of early humans, too. They're closer to your size!

Watch out! *Deinonychus* is one of the Peabody Museum's meat-eating dinosaurs.

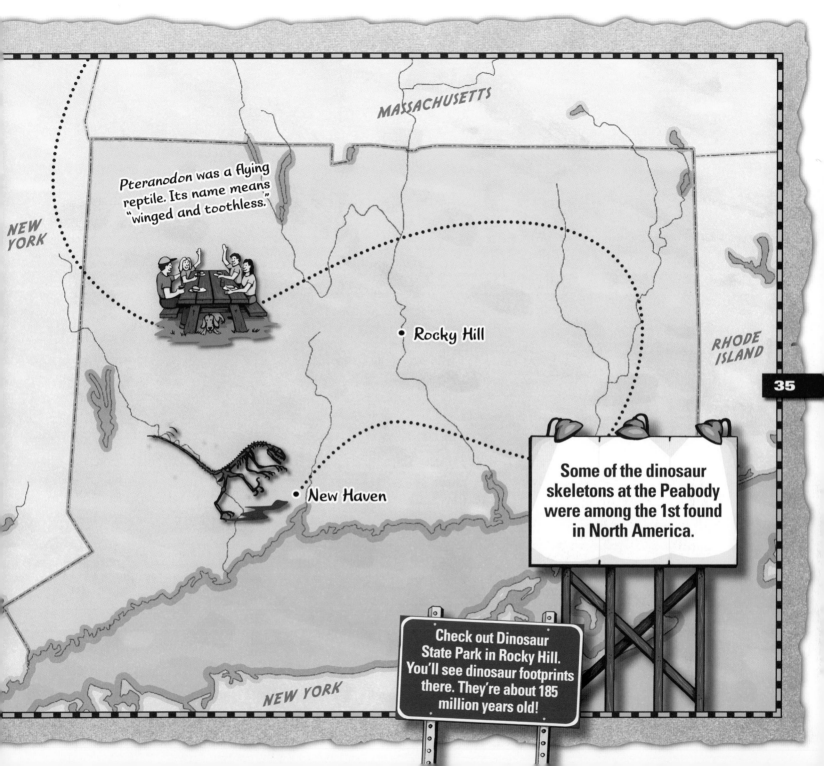

Pteranodon was a flying reptile. Its name means "winged and toothless."

Rocky Hill

New Haven

Some of the dinosaur skeletons at the Peabody were among the 1st found in North America.

Check out Dinosaur State Park in Rocky Hill. You'll see dinosaur footprints there. They're about 185 million years old!

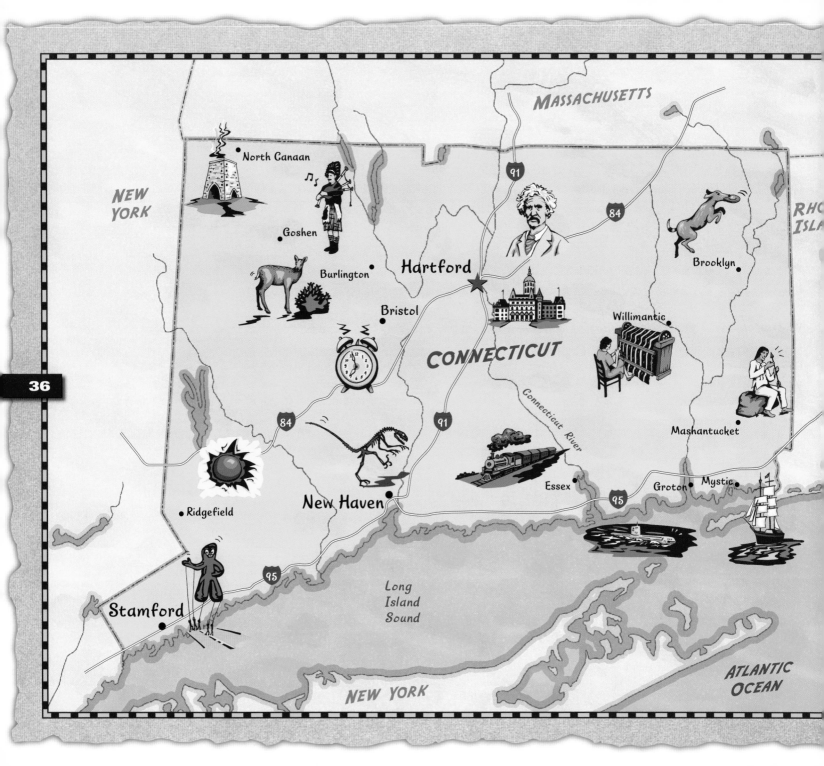

OUR TRIP

We visited many amazing places on our trip! We also met a lot of interesting people along the way. Look at the map on the left. Use your finger to trace all the places we have been.

Where is Heublein Tower located? See page 7 for the answer.

How many toes do black bears have on each foot? Page 8 has the answer.

Who fought in the Pequot War? See page 11 for the answer.

How old was Nathan Hale when he died? Look on page 12 for the answer.

What is haggis? Page 16 has the answer.

How hot did the Beckley Furnace get? Turn to page 20 for the answer.

What is the name of the last wooden whale ship? Look on page 22 and find out!

What can you see in the Yale-Harvard Regatta? Turn to page 27 for the answer.

WORDS TO KNOW

ammunition (am-yuh-NISH-uhn) objects such as bullets that are fired from guns

colonists (KOL-uh-nists) people who settle in a new land that is controlled by their home country

colony (KOL-uh-nee) a land with ties to a mother country

furnace (FUR-niss) a machine that burns fuel to create heat

immigrants (IM-uh-gruhnts) people who leave their home country and move to another land

industry (IN-duh-stree) a type of business

kilts (KILTS) men's clothing similar to skirts

nuclear (NOO-klee-ur) having to do with the energy inside tiny particles called atoms

tavern (TAV-urn) a public house where people can eat and drink

torpedo (tor-PEE-doh) an underwater weapon fired from a submarine

That was a great trip! We have traveled all over Connecticut!

There are a few places that we didn't have time for, though. Next time, we plan to visit Louis' Lunch in New Haven. The 1st hamburger was served there in 1900. You can still enjoy a juicy burger there today.

More Places to Visit in Connecticut

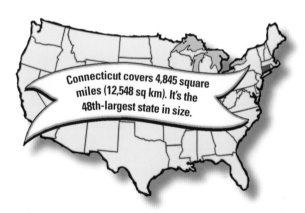

Connecticut covers 4,845 square miles (12,548 sq km). It's the 48th-largest state in size.

STATE SYMBOLS

State animal: Sperm whale

State bird: American robin

State composer: Charles Ives

State flower: Mountain laurel

State folk dance: Square dance

State fossil: *Eubrontes giganteus*

State hero: Nathan Hale

State heroine: Prudence Crandall

State insect: European mantis (praying mantis)

State mineral: Garnet

State shellfish: Eastern oyster

State ship: USS *Nautilus*

State tree: White oak

State seal

State flag

STATE SONG

"Yankee Doodle"
Traditional words and music

Yankee Doodle went to town,
Riding on a pony,
Stuck a feather in his hat,
And called it macaroni.

Chorus:
Yankee Doodle keep it up,
Yankee Doodle dandy,
Mind the music and the step,
And with the folks be handy.

FAMOUS PEOPLE

Arnold, Benedict (1741–1801), army officer, traitor

Barnum, P. T. (1810–1891), showman

Brown, John (1800–1859), abolitionist

Bush, George W. (1946–), 43rd U.S. president

Close, Glenn (1947–), actor

Colt, Samuel (1814–1862), inventor

Degen, Bruce (1945–), children's book illustrator

Falconer, Ian (1959–), children's author and illustrator

Goodyear, Charles (1800–1860), inventor

Grasso, Ella (1919–1981), 1st woman elected governor of a state

Hale, Nathan (1755–1776), American Revolutionary War hero

Hamill, Dorothy (1956–), figure skater

Hepburn, Katharine (1907–2003), actor

Leibovitz, Annie (1949–), photographer

Morgan, John Pierpont (1837–1913), banker and financier

Spock, Benjamin (1903–1998), pediatrician

Stowe, Harriet Beecher (1811–1896), author

Trumbull, John (1710–1785), merchant and politician

Twain, Mark (1835–1910), author

Webster, Noah (1758–1843), author of 1st American dictionary

TO FIND OUT MORE

At the Library
Burgan, Michael. *The Connecticut Colony.* Chanhassen, Minn.: The Child's World, 2003.

Grodin, Elissa, and Maureen K. Brookfield (illustrator). *N Is for Nutmeg: A Connecticut Alphabet.* Chelsea, Mich.: Sleeping Bear Press, 2003.

Streissguth, Tom, and Ralph Ramstad (illustrator). *John Brown.* Minneapolis: Carolrhoda Books, 1999.

Van Leeuwen, Jean, and Donna Diamond (illustrator). *Hannah's Helping Hands.* New York: Phyllis Fogelman Books, 1999.

Wyborny, Sheila. *Connecticut.* San Diego: Kidhaven Press, 2003.

On the Web
Visit our home page for lots of links about Connecticut:
http://www.childsworld.com/links

Note to Parents, Teachers, and Librarians: We routinely verify our Web links to make sure they are safe, active sites—so encourage your readers to check them out!

Places to Visit or Contact

The Connecticut Historical Society	Connecticut Office of Tourism
One Elizabeth Avenue	505 Hudson Street
Hartford, CT 06105	Hartford, CT 06106
860/236-5621	860/270-8080
For more information about the history of Connecticut	*For more information about traveling in Connecticut*

INDEX

Bye, Constitution State.
We had a great time.
We'll come back soon!